a special gift for

_____

from

_____

date

_____

hug's

Stories, sayings, and scriptures to Encourage and Inspire

to Brighten Your Day

ASHLEY MOORE &
KORIE ROBERTSON
Personalized Scriptures by
LEANN WEISS

HOWARD
PUBLISHING CO.

For Macy, Ally,
Maddox, John Luke,
Sadie, Will, and Bella—
our children,
who always brighten
our day.

Our purpose at Howard Publishing is to:

- *Increase faith* in the hearts of growing Christians
- *Inspire holiness* in the lives of believers
- *Instill hope* in the hearts of struggling people everywhere

Because He's coming again!

Contents

You are here
to enrich the world.

Woodrow Wilson

Reaching Out

• chapter one •

Reaching Out

Every day I am your way, your truth, and your life. You can reach out because I strengthen you in all you do. And as you give, watch Me multiply blessings back to you in overflowing ways.

Generously,
Your God of Every Good and Perfect Gift

—from John 14:6; Philippians 4:13; Luke 6:38; James 1:17

We all feel at times like we're running on a hamster wheel. Just running, around and around, with no end in sight. Today, though, you jumped off! You left the dishes piled in the sink and ran to a friend who needed a shoulder to cry on. Or maybe you left work early, even though your desk was covered with paperwork, to buy Christmas presents for kids at the battered women and children's shelter down the road.

Whatever it was you did for someone else, it felt good. You traded all the tasks on your to-do list for something of greater significance. And you noticed something. Nothing dreadful happened. The earth kept spinning on its axis. No natural disasters could be traced back to your change in schedule.

In fact, sometimes it's exactly when life seems to be spinning out of control—when you just don't think you could possibly help anybody else because your life is such a mess—it's exactly then that we need to reach out. Somehow you just do it, and afterward you know why it pays to go the extra mile.

Who knows but that you really needed that walk more than the person who asked you to join her. At any rate, it sure beats running on that wheel.

I have learned
that what we have done
for ourselves alone dies with us.
What we have done for others and
the world remains and is immortal.

❋

Albert Pike

This is only for a little while, Cheryl kept telling herself. But she was at the end of her rope.

The Gift

The phone rang as Cheryl was starting another load of laundry. It was the third one she'd done that day, along with cleaning the bathrooms, vacuuming the entire house, mopping the kitchen floor, and taking care of the three children—all while her husband sat in his home office leisurely working at the computer. Cheryl had thought Gary's going into

9

business for himself and having his office at home would be great for the family. But now she realized all that meant was that her husband never left work. Working was all he seemed to be doing these days.

"I'm not answering!" Cheryl hollered to Gary. "I don't have time to talk to anyone." She knew she sounded haggard. That was how she felt, and she wanted Gary to know it. Today was Saturday. She'd been trying to make her feelings known all week.

"Ring, ring, this is the Stone residence. Sorry we missed your call . . ." Cheryl could hear the answering machine from the hall. *Figures*, she thought. *Gary can't even take the time to answer the phone around here.* Then she muttered under her breath to whoever might be calling. "Don't hold your breath. 'As soon as possible' is gonna be a while."

Gary had decided to quit his job to become an independent contractor three months earlier with Cheryl's full support. He had plenty of computer expertise, and they felt confident he could get enough consulting work to make a good living. She just hadn't realized how hard he would have to work to make that happen.

For all her grumpiness, Cheryl knew Gary was a good

husband. He'd always participated fully with the three children, waking up for nighttime feedings when they were babies, taking turns shuttling the oldest to school and practice for whatever sport was in season. He'd stop by the grocery store or the pizza place on the way home from work to pick up supper, and he'd throw in a load or two of laundry when necessary. They had been a good team—always busy, but somehow it had worked. Until recently.

Cheryl understood that Gary was feeling the burden of responsibility to make it in his new venture and be able to support the family. *This is only for a little while, until he gets going,* she kept telling herself. But lately the positive self-talk was being drowned out by self-pity. *Sure, he's working, but I work full-time too, plus I'm doing everything else around here.* Their second-grader had homework at least a couple of nights a week, and the twin toddlers were a handful—the house seemed in a continual state of disaster. Cheryl was worn out and at the end of her rope. And when Gary didn't answer the phone, it felt like the last straw.

Her mental grumbling was interrupted by the voice on the answering machine. "Cheryl, this is Laura. I was hoping we could do something fun together this evening.

I really need a break from the hospital and could use someone to talk to."

Cheryl immediately felt awful. That was her best friend in the entire world. Laura's father had had a stroke on Monday. The doctors didn't think he would ever fully recover. Cheryl had gone to the hospital when it happened but had been so busy since then that she'd hardly even checked on Laura, except for one measly call to ask how her dad was doing.

I have to call her back, she thought, *but there's no way I can go.* There was more laundry to do, bills to pay, and groceries to shop for. Besides, who would watch the kids? If she left them home while Gary was working, they'd just destroy the house she'd worked all day to clean. She'd never get all the chores done before the new week started and they piled up all over again. She picked up the phone to somehow gracefully decline the invitation.

"When are you leaving?" Gary hollered.

"What do you mean, when am I leaving?" she retorted, not bothering to disguise her aggravation.

"I mean, I think you should go," Gary said with a smile as he joined her in the kitchen. "I'll stay home with the kids and keep the laundry going and do whatever else was on your list for the day."

"But what about your work?"

"It can wait. Your friend is more important. Besides, you need a little fun in your life too."

I couldn't agree more! she thought. "I don't know what's gotten into you, but I'll take you up on that offer!" Cheryl hugged her husband and happily picked up the phone to dial her best friend before he had a chance to change his mind.

After a quick conversation and a plan for Cheryl to pick up Laura at the hospital so they could ride together and talk on the way to the restaurant, Cheryl threw on

some lipstick, slipped on her boots, kissed the kids good-bye, and was out the door. She turned around quickly though, poked her head back inside, and yelled, "Don't forget to give the kids baths so they're clean for church in the morning." Her step was feeling a little lighter, but the knot in her stomach that had grown and tightened over the past few months was still there.

When she arrived at the hospital, Cheryl was struck by what a difficult thing Laura must be going through. She was an only child, and she had lost her mother just two years before. Somehow, though, Cheryl couldn't quite stop her mind from drifting back to her own problems.

"Thanks so much for rescuing me," Laura said as she met her friend at the front desk. "I can't tell you how much I needed this."

"Well, I have to admit, my life has been crazy lately, and getting away seemed almost too monumental a task when I first heard your message." Then, guiltily, "But I always have time for you."

As the two friends walked through the parking garage, the conversation kept going back to Cheryl and how stressful her situation was. She knew she should be letting her friend vent instead of complaining. But she couldn't

14

stop worrying about whether her husband was really doing what he said he would or if he had slipped back to his office. She was going to lose it if she came home to a houseful of chores and dirty children.

As they approached the car, she noticed Laura looking in the window of an old, brown Chevy Caprice that had definitely seen better days. Cheryl muttered an attempt at humor, "I think they need to haul that clunker off to the junkyard."

But Laura didn't laugh. She started rummaging in her overcrowded purse. Cheryl saw her friend pull out a paper from her wallet and lean into the open window of the "clunker."

"Oh!" Cheryl stuttered. "I—I hope I didn't offend you by making fun of that car. Were you leaving a note for someone you know?"

"No," Laura replied somewhat mysteriously. "Come on; let's go enjoy a wonderful meal. I'm sick of hospital food."

But Cheryl's curiosity was aroused. She came around to where Laura was standing and peeked into the window of the old car. A bright yellow notice with a red FINAL stamp on it was lying face-up on the seat. It was an electric bill for $98.99. Then something else caught her eye.

Tucked under that notice, just barely showing, was the corner of what looked like money.

Cheryl knew instantly what Laura had done. Her friend had always been kind-hearted, but seeing her do something that generous in the midst of such a difficult time in her life brought tears to Cheryl's eyes. *What a contrast to my wallowing in self-pity*, she thought, ashamed. Today, while she'd been busy thinking only of herself, her husband had set aside what he was doing and thought of her. And her friend, who was in the midst of her own turmoil, had listened to Cheryl's little grievances and helped someone she didn't even know. It was a living illustration of how to set aside her problems and think of someone else.

She turned and hugged Laura as tightly as she could. "Thanks, Laura."

"For what? I didn't give *you* the money," Laura joked.

"For reminding me how truly blessed I am."

Looking Up

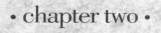

· chapter two ·

Looking Up

Get the right perspective by looking up and remembering that I'm your power source. I'm watching over you and won't let you slip or fall. Nothing is too difficult for Me. Wait upon Me, and I'll renew you and help you to soar above the obstacles of life so you won't quit.

Encouraging you,
Your Heavenly Father

—*from Psalm 121:2–5; Luke 1:37; Isaiah 40:31*

You give it all you've got. But in this world, all you've got isn't always good enough. Except with those who love you. For them your best is better than good enough. It's perfect!

There's something you don't hear very often. You, perfect? Well, in a way you are. Not that you always succeed or never make mistakes. But you're perfect in the sense that you're just the way God made you. Perfect, not because of anything you've done, but because you are the person He created you to be. And what does He ask for in return? That you keep trying. That you do your best and look to Him when you need help.

Sometimes relying on someone else is easier said than done. You've worked hard, and it's difficult to admit you need help. You're strong, self-sufficient. You want to stand on your own two feet. And that's good. All parents want their children to grow into strong, independent adults. Your heavenly Father is no different.

Just remember that like a loving parent, He also wants to be there for you. He's cheering for you. And He's waiting for your glance—ready for the time you look up to heaven, telling Him you need Him. Until then, He'll wait. He won't take His eyes off of you.

We bring nothing to God,
and He gives us everything.

Gary Thomas

Robert stood there,

longing for his

daughter to give him

just one glance.

Out of the Sand

Robert's stomach was in knots. Watching his daughter bound down the runway to leap with all her might into the soft sand, he couldn't help but wonder how she was handling the pressure. She had told him coming home from regionals that when she jumped, the sand didn't feel soft at all; it felt like freshly poured concrete that had almost completely set up.

She had worked hard, training endlessly for today's event—the state track meet. This was Erin's senior year, her last chance, and her dream was there for the taking. Robert wanted his daughter to succeed, to achieve what she'd worked so hard for. He'd coached and encouraged her along the way, but now there was nothing more he could do. He and his wife, Karen, could only stand there, knuckles white, grasping the yellow guard rail as Erin ran for her first jump.

She did it! It looked good enough to Robert. Karen jumped up and down with pride and excitement. Although it was hard to tell from their place in the stands, he could see the beaming face of their only child and knew it must have been a good jump.

But her body language was saying something different. Instead of her usual dancelike bound as she rose from the sand, Erin was moving slowly. This was not a good sign.

"I think she's hurt," Karen said. Robert saw it too; he responded with a silent mix of hope and concern. Erin had two more jumps to go, and while no one but her parents would have noticed, they could tell something wasn't right.

Erin was in second place at the end of round one, and Robert thought about the many times she had won after a more meager start. But watching his daughter's broken steps

26

as she prepared for her second attempt, Robert's fears were confirmed. Erin was hurting.

"Erin Thompson up!" rang out from the loud speaker. As she ran down the runway, Robert rocked from side to side, feeling with his daughter each painful step.

She made the jump, but this time there was no smile— and certainly no bounce after her accomplishment. "Fourteen feet seven inches," the judge announced. Not as long as the first. Erin jammed her right hand into the sand and pushed herself up. Robert recognized the grim determination he'd often seen in his daughter.

"She's a fighter," Karen said under her breath, putting into words what Robert was thinking.

He laughed. "Remember when she was two? Her favorite phrase was 'I do it myself!'" Robert was proud of Erin's strength but always wished she would lean on him and her mother at least a little. He stood there longing for his daughter to give him just one small glance, to look his way so he could tell her with his eyes just how proud he was of her, no matter what she did or what place she finished.

While most of the crowd talked and laughed, Robert stood statuesque, never taking his eyes off his daughter. If she should happen to look his way, he'd give her a big smile and a thumbs up to let her know he was there if she needed him.

"Round three! Erin Thompson up!" The call came all too quickly. Erin started down the runway, focused on the goal. Robert was focused on her. He nearly threw himself over the rail as she made the final jump. "Fourteen feet and five inches!" the judge yelled.

That may have been good enough for regionals, but it won't cut it for state, Robert thought. His heart sank, knowing how disappointed Erin would be.

"Top six to the finals, listen carefully for the names," the judge said. "Julia Jackson, Carmen Smith, Amy Rodgers, Samantha Kennedy, Casey Gaston, and in sixth place, Erin Thompson. You have thirty minutes to prepare."

Erin had never been in sixth place in anything her whole life. Robert saw the anger and disbelief on his daughter's face. Yet still no glance for which Robert longed as he watched his little girl limp the entire length of the track to the field house.

"I hate this," he told his wife.

"She'll be fine," she tried to assure him.

"I can't take it anymore," he said. "I'm going out there."

"Robert—"

Out of the Sand

The rest of Karen's words were lost. He was already halfway across the stands. His imagination was getting the better of him as he envisioned finding his daughter in tears. Then he spotted her. In the far right-hand corner of the crowded room, hidden behind the leg press machine, Erin was trying to stretch out. Robert could see that she couldn't bend down far on her left leg, but he saw no sign of defeat on Erin's face. She was set like stone.

He stood back for a moment, marveling at her valiant struggle to overcome the pain. He smiled and decided to leave her to her preparation. Just as he started to go, Erin's eyes met his.

"I can do this, Dad."

He nodded. "I know."

Robert walked back to the stands, his steps a little lighter. At

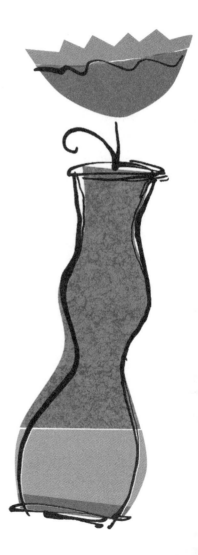

least he had made contact. Erin knew he was there for her if she needed him.

He slid back into his seat beside Karen just in time to hear the voice from the loud speaker. "Girls' long jump!" His stomach tightened again as six athletically lean girls walked to the runway. One had a look of elation, another seemed pensive, but Erin had that familiar stare of pride and determination as she limped all the way.

Erin started warming up, and Robert rose from his seat to assume his guardian stance. Karen stood beside him. "Has it been thirty minutes already?"

"I don't think she's ready," Robert muttered.

"She was born ready," was Karen's confident reply. Robert smiled, knowing she was right.

"Erin Thompson up!"

Even before the judge's announcement, Robert knew Erin's jump hadn't been long enough.

"Thirteen feet ten inches!"

His heart broke for his daughter, but he couldn't see any break in her spirit. She pounded both hands into the grainy sand and sprang up, using only her right foot to carry the weight of her slender body.

Out of the Sand

"Come on, Erin, you can do it!" Robert yelled, hoping she would hear him and look up for a little support. But if Erin was listening, she didn't let on. She simply resumed her stretches, readying herself for the next jump.

Her distance was only getting lower, and this time Erin had to practically crawl out of the sand. It was almost too much to bear. She only had one more chance.

As all the other contestants went bounding down the runway one after another, Robert wished he could take this pressure away from his daughter, make it all better. Hug her and tell her it was fine, he loved her no matter what. If she didn't want to jump again, it was OK. This was just a silly competition—it didn't really matter.

But he knew it did. Erin had worked hard for this, and nothing was going to keep her from giving her best—even if today her best wouldn't win a medal.

Erin slumped on the black asphalt, waiting her turn. "Just look at me, honey," Robert pleaded under his breath, hoping to pass her some kind of support from across the field.

The loud speaker blared. "This is your final jump. Erin Thompson up!"

Erin struggled to her place, and just before getting set, she looked up into the stands. Robert read her meaning. She knew they were there for her, and she was going to give it her all. He blinked to hide the mistiness of his eyes and stood grinning, cheering her on. "That's my girl!" he yelled. "Give 'em all you've got."

Her best had always been enough for him. But would it be enough for his competitive daughter? One last time, Erin took off down the runway, awkwardly striving for her goal.

"Thirteen feet even."

It was short. But this time there was no hand-pounding. There was no movement to get up from the sand. Just a slow turn of the head to search out her father, looking for help. She needed him.

Out of the Sand

Robert hurdled the cold, yellow guard rail and sprinted to Erin's side. Tears of pain streaked her cheeks. Robert knelt and gently lifted her out of the sand. "I'm proud of you," he whispered in her ear. "Are you all right?"

"Of course I am. I did my best, and a girl can't do any better than that," Erin said proudly, though Robert could hear the pain in her voice.

"I knew that, but I wasn't sure if you knew it."

"Hey, what have you been teaching me all these years?" Erin said with a half-smile, half-grimace.

"That's my girl," Robert said unevenly, his voice betraying the depth of emotion and pride he felt. "That's my girl."

Making a Difference

chapter three

Making a Difference

35

Come to Me when you
need a pick-me-up,
and I'll refresh you and
teach you balance. I'm
able to make all grace
abound to you so that in
all things at all times,
you'll have all the
resources you need to
excel in every good work
I've planned for you.

Energizing you,
Your God of Power

—from Matthew 11:28–30; 2 Corinthians 9:8

What would happen if you just didn't get out of bed this morning? Oh, maybe that call to the client wouldn't have been made or the closet would still be a mess. But more importantly, would you have been missed?

Have you ever gone on vacation and realized it took four people to do what you do on a normal day? Your friend drove the carpool and took the older kids to baseball practice, your mom picked up your toddler from daycare, your coworker answered your calls and took care of necessary business, and your dad watered your plants and fed your pets. It takes a lot of people to fill in for you.

You are valuable, but not just for those daily chores everyone takes for granted that you'll take care of. You are valuable for being you.

When you're gone, you're missed because you are a positive force in the lives of those around you. You make your child's day with the little notes you leave in his lunchbox. Your coworkers love to see your smiling face. Your husband needs your encouraging words and a kiss on the cheek after a long day.

That's why you do it. That's why even when life gets tough, or when for whatever reason you're just plain tired, you keep going. You get out of bed, you start your day, and you bless others with your presence. You hold an important place in their hearts. Because whatever tasks they perform, no one else can be you.

Let no man imagine
that he has no influence.
Whoever he may be, and wherever
he may be placed, the man who thinks
becomes a light and a power.

✳

Henry George

Kim could hardly bring

herself to get out of bed.

She never thought

this could happen to her.

Back to School

Kim Matheny's alarm screamed in her ears. Although she knew it was time to get up, the thirty-five-year-old kindergarten teacher lay motionless, head still swimming from the recent turn of events. It had been just seven days since she received the devastating news. She had cancer.

She'd spent the previous week away from her classroom in a

whirlwind of doctor visits, Internet research, and life-or-death decisions. Today was Monday, and she was due back at school. Although she loved her students dearly, she could hardly bring herself to get out of bed, let alone face their questions about why she'd been gone, what was cancer, was she going to die.

Kim forced herself to sit up, knowing she had to keep moving to ward off the looming depression over her diagnosis. She never thought this could happen to her, but reminded herself that no one ever does, and wondered how the kids would handle her illness.

Maybe another teacher would be better for them. No, I'd miss them too much. But what if teaching is more than I can handle right now? I need their cheery faces and sweet hugs. She plopped back down, thoughts racing and panic rising. *What if they've already gotten used to the substitute and don't care if I come back? Kids forget quickly. Maybe I don't matter as much as I think—*

"Stop it!" She scolded herself aloud. "Get a grip." She slammed the snooze button again and let her arm just drop onto the nightstand. Her hand landed on a colorful note she had received the day before.

She picked it up and unfolded it again. The drawing was

of a rainbow, a bright yellow sun, and two stick figures. The larger one was labeled "Ms. Mateny" and the smaller one "Me." One figure's arm reached out toward the other's, and the two lines were joined at the bottom with one large, round scribble representing the holding of hands. Then, in purple crayon, "You briten my day, Ms. Mateny. I miss you. Come back soon." It was signed "Luv, Macy." Tears filled Kim's eyes. *My kids need me.* She got out of bed to get ready for school.

On the drive to Southwood Elementary, Kim thought of numerous ways to greet her class. Her usual song, "It's a beautiful day, it's a beautiful day, the birds are singing, let's shout hooray," didn't seem fitting. The sun was shining and the birds were singing, but she just didn't think she could form those words on her lips today.

The thirty-minute drive and her walk to the classroom seemed to drift by in a fog. Kim usually was in high gear before class, adjusting the weather chart and setting out the first activity to make sure everything was ready when the students arrived. Today she sat at her desk, perfectly still except for the distracted tapping of her pencil on a stack of papers.

"Hi, Kim." The sympathetic tone belonged to Sarah

Richardson, who taught the first-grade class across the hall. "The children will be here shortly. If you need anything today, please come and get me."

Kim looked at her friend nervously. "I don't know if I can do this."

Sarah nodded assurance. "You'll make it. And like I said, I'm here if you need me."

The kind support nearly shattered Kim's resolve not to cry, but she swallowed hard and blinked to clear her eyes. "Thanks."

One by one the children began arriving. Samuel, always eager for school, came running in first. "Ms. Matheny, what are we doing today?" It didn't seem he'd even noticed her weeklong absence.

Kim was disappointed but tried not to let it show. "We have a lot planned for today. I'm so glad you're excited about school," she said with all the enthusiasm she could muster. Her one buoy—the special place she thought she had in her students' hearts—was sinking fast. Had the children even missed her at all?

Nathan arrived next, clutching his mother's pant leg as he used to do. Kim had made such progress with him, but now he treated her like a stranger again.

46

"He was like this all last week," Nathan's mother said.

"Oh, Nathan." Kim gently rubbed his back, trying to ease her own anxiety as much as his. Had she lost all the ground she had gained since the beginning of the school year? She just didn't have the heart to start over. "I'm so glad you're here. I sure need my little helper today." Her voice quavered a little, and she stopped, afraid she'd be completely engulfed by discouragement.

Then suddenly Nathan released his mother's leg and turned for his teacher to pick him up.

As Kim hugged him tightly, he whispered, "I'm so glad you're back."

Next came Sadie. She didn't say a word, but her dimples flashed as she embraced her teacher shyly before scurrying to her desk.

47

The rest of the class had arrived, but where was Macy? She usually arrived about twenty minutes early to help Kim by setting out scissors or crayons or whatever she asked her to do. Macy hadn't missed a day of school all year. She loved being there and always had a smile to share with a friend. Kim suddenly realized just how much she'd missed Macy's good cheer during the most difficult week of her life. She needed Macy to be there today.

Just as Kim was calling the class to attention, Macy walked into the classroom slowly, with her head down. Not even a hint of the smile Kim so desperately needed. Her spirits sank to a new low. Was Macy not even happy to have her back? Near tears, Kim forced herself to try to sound cheery.

"Well hello, Macy!"

Macy jerked to attention, looking up for the first time since she'd entered the room.

"Ms. Matheny! It's you!" Macy squealed with delight, running to squeeze her teacher's leg as tightly as she could.

"Of course, it's me," Kim giggled, bending to return the hug and thank Macy for her wonderful note.

"I didn't think you were coming back." Macy's eyes were

as round and bright as the big yellow sun she had drawn on her picture.

"Yes, Macy, I'm back. I need you little munchkins. Did you miss me?" Kim asked hopefully.

Macy made a face and answered almost indignantly. "Yes! Who else would teach us to count and write and color?"

"Who'd teach us those silly songs?" another student joined in earnestly.

"Who would tell us who gets to be the line leader or the door holder? That other teacher didn't know anything about that," Samuel added.

"I'm sure your substitute teacher was very good," Kim protested—but not too strongly. She was enjoying this outpouring of affection.

"Not near as good as you," Sadie countered.

"Yeah," Macy said adamantly. "And no one can give hugs as good as you!"

At this the entire class ran to the front of the classroom, nearly tackling their beloved teacher as they jostled to get one of her warm hugs and to give one in return.

"Well!" Sarah interrupted from the doorway, smiling

approvingly at her friend. "I guess you have everything under control."

Kim laughed. "I don't know about that. But I know this is exactly where I needed to be today. I think we'll be just fine."

"I know you will," Sarah responded confidently.

Cherishing Old Friends

· chapter four ·

Cherishing Old Friends

I've called you My friend. I've chosen you and appointed you to make a lasting difference. Loving each other is what counts! Friends love at all times and help each other in the hard times.

Loving you always,
Your Friend and King

—from John 15:15–17; Proverbs 17:17

"Make new friends but keep the old. One is silver and the other gold." It's an old song, but it rings even more true today than when you first learned it. Now you understand it.

It's great to make new friends, but friendships that have withstood the test of time are priceless. There's nothing better than having a friend who was in the waiting room when you delivered your first baby and then again when your husband was in the ICU. Someone who really listens when you need to talk, who will meet you at the mall when you need a break from your daily routine, who doesn't notice if your house is a mess when she drops by to say hello.

Jesus said, "Greater love has no one than this, that he lay down his life for his friends" (John 15:13). Wow. That's a friend indeed.

Most of us don't have occasion to literally lay down our lives for our friends. But we can lay down our lives every day, in a million little ways. We can break through our self-protection to share life's deepest struggles and joys. We can sacrifice the "important" things we had to do today to spend time with a friend who's lonely. We can take a few minutes to write a note or give a hug to a friend who's done such things for us.

Old friends, like gold, are treasures. Let them know they're cherished.

That best portion of a good man's life,
[are] His little nameless
unremembered acts of kindness
and love.

✻

William Wordsworth

Charles knew he was disappointing his friends, but it wasn't just the arthritis holding him back.

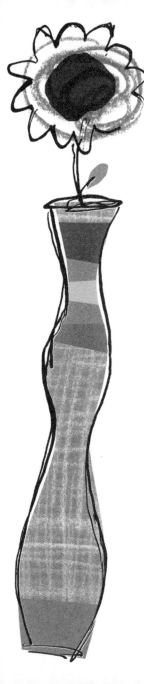

Fore!

"I'm not sure if I'm going to make it this year." Charles grimaced as he said this into the phone. He knew it wouldn't be taken well.

"What are you talking about?" David responded. "It's a tradition, Charles, you have to be there."

Charles didn't know how he was going to handle being at home on this third weekend in July, the weekend his three closest

59

friends would be at the Iron Horse Golf Course in Texas just as they had been for the past fifty-four years. He was the one who'd started this tradition. But he simply couldn't handle going either. He'd thought about it a lot. This would be best.

"David, you know how much I love seeing you guys, but I just can't play anymore. My arthritis has gotten so bad that I'd be in bed for a week if I even tried to swing a club."

"So come and just ride in the cart. We want you to be there."

"I'll think about it," Charles said, but he'd already made up his mind that the trip would be too hard. It wasn't just the arthritis holding him back.

Mary had died in January, and he hadn't gotten out much since then. This year the third weekend in July was not only the golf reunion date; that Sunday would have been his and Mary's anniversary.

The tradition had gotten its start the weekend of their wedding. Each of these guys had been groomsmen, and they played golf the day before the ceremony. They'd come back every year since.

This had drawn a few complaints from Mary over the

years, when the calendar rotation meant he was gone on their anniversary. But she never really minded. She knew how much his friends meant to him, and they always made sure to take a trip or do something special together the weekend before.

"Well, I don't know what we are going to do without you," Dave said. "It just won't be the same." They said their good-byes.

❋

"Edwin, can you believe he's not coming?" David said into the phone. He had immediately dialed Edwin's number after talking with Charles. He knew Edwin would have a solution. He'd always been the leader of the group, which was probably precisely why Charles had not broken the news to him. *Edwin wouldn't have let him off the hook so easily*, David thought, kicking himself for not saying the right thing.

The two friends agreed that this had to be a rough year for Charles, and they understood his grief at his first anniversary without his wife. But it seemed to them the worst thing he

could do was stay at home, alone. They wanted to be there to support him during this time. That's what friends were for, after all. But just how were they going to convince Charles to join them?

"I can't believe he used the arthritis as an excuse," Edwin said. "He should know I'll never let him get away with that. Remember the year I broke my leg and still came, cast and all?"

David laughed and cringed. "Yeah, you nearly broke your other leg trying to swing a club while balancing on the one good leg!"

Edwin chuckled, then sighed. "I'll call John. He's been through this. It's only been three years since Lisa passed away, maybe he can encourage Charles and convince him to come."

Fore!

✳

"He is not changing his mind," John told Edwin a week later, after many phone calls between the four friends. "I've tried everything, and I can't convince him. He's afraid he'll be too sad, between thoughts of Mary and being stuck riding in the cart, unable to play. Said he'd just bring us all down and none of us would have any fun."

"Well, that beats all," Edwin said. There was a pause, then he continued decisively. "I won't have it. We can't let him sit at home because he's worried about ruining the trip for us. We'll just have to go get him."

"That would be the only way to get him there," John agreed, not sure if his friend was serious.

"I mean it, John. We'll show up at his doorstep and drag him to the course." Edwin had spoken. Their course was set.

"This won't be easy since he lives at least three states away from any of us." John grinned, knowing full well Edwin would pull it off even though their work and families had spread them each to a different part of the country.

✳

63

"This is not a good day for company," Charles grumbled as the doorbell rang again.

He hadn't gotten any sleep the night before, tossing and turning with grief for his wife and regret at his decision to stay home on this weekend. He knew he was disappointing his friends. They had all come in for the funeral, and it had meant the world to him. Maybe he should go. He hadn't booked a plane ticket though, so it really was out of the question.

I could just get in the car and start driving, he thought. It was Thursday afternoon, and Charles had been thinking about that option all morning. His friends would all be flying into town on Friday. He could make it if he started driving by dinnertime.

Or maybe he had made the right decision. He'd be terrible company like this. They counted on him to keep everyone laughing. He'd always been the fun guy. But not this year. He didn't want his friends to see him like this. Maybe after he got past the hurdle of this first year. Maybe he'd be back next year.

Charles's mind was still in turmoil as he shuffled reluctantly to the door and opened it.

"FORE!" Edwin, David, and John shouted in unison.

Fore!

Charles just stood there, mouth agape, as his friends all began talking at once, each saying how much their longtime friend meant to them and vowing not to leave until he had packed his bags and agreed to come along.

"Oh yeah," Edwin said. "And can we take your car?"

They all burst into laughter, and Charles was glad to have an excuse for the moistening in his eyes.

"It'll be a road trip, just like in our college days," Edwin said with a twinkle in his eyes. "We'll even stop to buy you those pink snowball things you always liked to eat."

"How can I say no to snowballs?" Charles said, all hesitation gone. "I'll go pack my bags."

"Get your clubs too," David shouted after him. "Yours are a lot better than mine, and if you're just going to be sitting in the cart, I might as well put them to good use."

Charles returned with a small duffel bag of clothes, his golf bag, and tears in his eyes. He'd decided there was no use trying to hide anything from such good friends. "Thanks, guys. You'll never know how much I needed you to walk through that door when you did."

"That's what friends are for," Edwin said, slapping him gently on the back. "That's what friends are for."

Enjoying Surprises

· chapter five ·

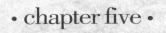
Enjoying Surprises

Experience My abundant
life! I'm continuing to
work behind the scenes
on your behalf, and I
love to far exceed your
expectations and dreams.
Taste and see My goodness
in your life.

Blessing you,
Your God of Wonder

—from John 10:10; Ephesians 3:20; Psalm 34:8

Surprise! Have you ever heard that word shouted by a large group of friends and family? It's so much fun! Kids young and old love a surprise party. Everyone comes abuzz with anticipation, chattering about how they almost slipped and gave away the secret or wondering if the surprisee suspects anything.

Perhaps the only feeling more exciting than receiving such a surprise is perpetrating one. Planning a big surprise makes you feel great, doesn't it? You can't help but tingle with excitement. In fact, you realize, you've smiled more in the days leading up to the event than you have all year!

Sure, some people aren't comfortable with parties, but don't believe it when they tell you they don't like surprises. Whatever form it takes, we all like to have something special done for us. Something thoughtful, be it big or small, that we didn't have to lift a finger for and that we never expected.

Why are surprises so great? Because when someone surprises you with a party, a single flower on your desk, or a sparkling clean house, it means that someone thought of you, cared about your happiness so much that he or she did something just for you.

If you haven't surprised anyone lately, even with something little, it's time. Choose someone you love, put in a little thought and planning, and just do it. You'll both be surprised at how good it feels.

Into all our lives, in many simple,
familiar, homely ways, God infuses this
element of joy from the surprises of life,
which unexpectedly brighten our days
and fill our eyes with light.

❋

Samuel Longfellow

Cynthia had been longing

for a romantic getaway.

Going fishing

wasn't Hawaii, but

it was something.

The Fishing Trip

"Thank you so much, Kathy, for taking care of the kids today," Cynthia said as she and Tom dropped off their children at her best friend's house.

"No problem. You two have a good time," Kathy responded, shooing the couple out the door.

"Bye, darlings. You be sweet. We'll be back after dinner." Cynthia gave each child a kiss on

75

the top of the head. The children giggled and hugged their mom tightly.

"Kathy seems almost as excited about our anniversary as we are!" Cynthia remarked as they walked back to the car.

Four children between the ages of eight and two didn't leave Tom and Cynthia much time alone together, but today was their tenth anniversary, and they were going to the lake and then out to dinner. Cynthia had hoped for more, but this would be nice, and she had resigned herself to the fact that this was all they could do.

Off and on throughout the year, Cynthia had been thinking back to their honeymoon. It had been a dream vacation to Hawaii, and they had stayed at a beautiful resort—before dirty diapers and middle-of-the-night feedings took over. That was the last time she and Tom had taken a trip together, and she wanted so badly to do something really special for their tenth anniversary.

She wasn't complaining, really. She enjoyed their full life. They'd both wanted a house full of children, and it didn't take long before they had gotten their wish. A family that large, though, did pose some challenges. Just planning a "date night" every once in a while was a task, much less actually going away for a weekend. Anyway, by the time

76

they got four kids through diapers, formula, doctor visits, and piano lessons, the extra money for a vacation was just never there.

Still, ever since their youngest child was weaned off the bottle, Cynthia had been longing for a getaway. She was ready to put some focus back on her and Tom again, to do something fun and exciting that didn't involve kids. She'd dropped several hints about how great it would be to recapture those romantic moments from their honeymoon, to actually sleep with just the two of them in the bed without one or two little bodies sneaking in during the middle of the night.

Cynthia had even gathered information on cruises and trips to the beach and left them lying around for Tom to see. But they couldn't do it, Tom had told her. They just didn't have the extra funds.

"You're right," she had said with a sigh. "Besides, what would we do with the kids? It would be a nightmare trying to find someone to keep them. And ugh," she'd gone on, trying to be a good sport, "just the thought of packing for all of them!"

So they had decided to go fishing. It wasn't Hawaii, but it was something she and Tom had loved doing together when they were dating and newly married. They still took the kids fishing fairly often, but it was always a major effort to get them all packed up. Then they spent most of their time putting fresh bait on each child's hook after the fish had nibbled it away without ever biting into the hook. Cynthia was looking forward to this more relaxed outing.

"This will be fun," she said with a smile, leaning over in the suburban to give her husband a kiss on the cheek as they pulled out of her friend's driveway.

Tom seemed glad for the break too. "Yeah, it's just you and me, baby. Are you sure you're OK with the fact that we didn't get to go on that dream vacation?"

"Oh, sure. Just spending the day with you will be great," she reassured him. "But for our twentieth anniversary, I'm expecting no less than the Bahamas!"

Tom laughed. "All right, I promise."

"Where do you want to eat tonight?" Cynthia asked absentmindedly as she settled back to enjoy the ride.

"Oh, I don't care. You might want to wait and decide that when we get there."

Cynthia thought she caught a bit of mischief in his tone. It was the way he used to sound when he had a fun secret. "When we get where?" she asked, sitting up straight. Tom broke into a full grin. Something was up.

"You'll see," he replied teasingly. "Just sit back and relax. Your only job for the next few days is to enjoy yourself."

"Few days! Did you say *few days?*" Cynthia squealed, a fresh sparkle in her eyes.

"It will all be clear soon enough," he insisted. Just a few hundred yards later, he took the exit ramp that read Airport.

"No way!" Cynthia exclaimed. "Really, are we going to the airport?"

"Fasten your safety belt and put your tray tables in the locked position," Tom joked, passing her a note.

Cynthia couldn't unfold the paper fast enough. On it was a handwritten poem. Tom had written her many poems, but recently

they'd become few and far between. He wasn't very good at poetry, to be honest—his were usually pretty corny. But Cynthia didn't care. They were always funny and warm, and she had saved every one. She read aloud:

To my wife of ten amazing years,
I love you more each day.
That's why I wanted to surprise you
In this very special way.
Today I hope to fulfill your dream
And fill your heart with joy;
I'm taking you on a trip to Cancun,
Now come here and kiss this boy!
It's you and me, babe, for five nights and days,
To do whatever we wish:
Take walks on the beach or naps in our room,
Who knows—we might even fish.
The kids are in good hands,
You're mom's on her way.
You're bag is packed, our room is booked,
So let's go! What do you say?

The Fishing Trip

Cynthia brushed away a tear and laughed. She suddenly felt lighter than air. "I say you're the greatest husband in the whole world!" She nearly caused a fender-bender smothering Tom with kisses as he pulled into a parking space at the airport.

She couldn't stop smiling as she got out of the car. As she walked toward the back of the vehicle, she saw Tom unloading their suitcases, which had been hidden under a blanket behind the backseat. "Oh, no, how in the world did you know what to pack?"

"Kathy came over yesterday while you took Aaron to baseball practice. If we forgot anything, I guess we'll just have to buy it there."

"Did you happen to forget my swimsuit? I could use a new one," Cynthia said with a sly grin.

Tom smiled back. "You can buy whatever you want. I've been saving for this trip for a while now."

Cynthia was stunned. "OK, I've always thought you were the greatest husband—now I know you are!" She gave him a long kiss.

As they walked up to the ticket counter hand in hand, pulling their luggage behind them, Cynthia was reminded again of what had made her fall in love with Tom in the first place. He made the little things, the day-to-day stuff, seem special—and the big things absolutely wonderful. He must have worked hard to plan this little surprise. She was looking forward to hearing her mom and the kids and Kathy tell all about how they had kept the big secret and pulled this off. But for now, at last, it was just the two of them heading off to a "fishing trip" she knew she'd never forget.

Believing the Best

• chapter six •

Believing the Best

You can always count
on Me to fulfill all of
My promises to you.
My faithfulness is guar-
anteed. I'm always for
you! Nothing can ever
separate you from My love.

Hugs,

Your Promise Keeper

—from Psalms 145:13; 100:5; Romans 8:31, 38–39

"You can't do that!" "There's no way!" "Just forget it!" "You're way too busy!" Ever heard those objections? Unfortunately, sometimes they come from inside our own heads.

Some people, though, never seem to let those thoughts cross their minds. They're the ones who say there's no such thing as "can't." And they seem to have all the fun. They take skydiving lessons, go on safaris in the jungles of Africa, or invent solutions to "unsolvable" problems.

They aren't rich, necessarily—not just the beautiful people or the smartest or the most talented. Their secret isn't what they have or do or are. It's how they think.

They believe.

They believe they can do anything they put their minds to and that nothing will happen to them that they can't rise above.

They believe worry is wasteful and know that if they just keep going, things will work out in the end.

And they believe persevering through trials develops strength and endurance, empowering them for the next great adventure—or the next challenge.

What separates these can-do people who live fulfilling, fantastic lives from the rest of us? Nothing, really, if you just believe.

Nothing we do,
however virtuous,
can be accomplished alone;
therefore, we are saved by love.

✳

Reinhold Niebuhr

Luke shot a look
at his wife. He had no
intention of obeying
the doctor's orders.

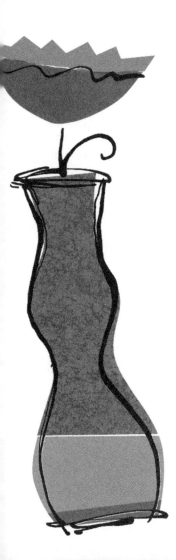

Wouldn't Miss It

A groan escaped Luke's lips as pain shot through his knee. After a restless night of sleep, he'd awakened to realize the injury that he was hoping would simply go away was not only present but getting worse. His wife of forty-eight years, who apparently wasn't sleeping either, asked, "How does it feel? Do you need something?"

"Now, Jo, I'm going to be fine. There's nothing to worry about."

His protective wife didn't seem convinced. "I'm calling Dr. Brown this morning to make you an appointment."

"For heaven's sake, Jo, I don't need to see a doctor." He tried to shrug it off. "I have an important meeting at the office today, and you know Brianna's big game is tonight. I'm not going to let a little fall put a hold on my life."

"Who's talking about stopping your life, and what do you mean 'little fall'? Jack told me how hard you fell on that tile floor yesterday."

Luke slapped his hand over his forehead and slid it down to cover his eyes. "Oh, don't even mention the other realtors. That was so embarrassing. They probably think I'm getting feeble."

"They do not, Luke. But you have to face facts; you're seventy-five years old, and your knee is swollen to the size of a grapefruit." She took on the emphatic tone Luke knew it was useless to fight against. "You are going to the doctor today."

He gently lowered his swollen leg to the floor and let out an even louder groan. Jo got up as well and headed toward the kitchen.

Wouldn't Miss It

"I haven't started the coffee this morning. I guess I over-slept," Luke called out. The truth was, he'd woken thirty minutes earlier but was in so much pain he wasn't sure he could even stand, much less go through his morning routine. For the last forty-eight years, he'd had a fresh pot of coffee waiting for Jo every morning, and he knew this small gesture left undone would give away just how bad his knee really was. He needed to downplay his injury just a little longer.

"I've taught all of my children and grandchildren from the time they were little that when you make a promise, you keep it," Luke hollered to Jo from the bathroom. "And I don't plan to start breaking my promises just because of a sore knee." Especially this one. He'd promised Brianna he wouldn't miss any of her basketball games this season. This was her senior year, and her team had made the playoffs. He wasn't about to miss what could be her final game.

"Luke, dear," his wife called back, "we'll discuss it after we see what the doctor says. I just spoke to Dr. Brown's office, and they can get you in later this morning."

"But my meeting with the new realtors is at eleven o'clock."

"I've already called the office, and everyone will be notified that the meeting is being rescheduled. Now let me help you get dressed."

"OK, I'll go," Luke consented, mostly for show. Jo obviously wasn't making this optional. "And I can get dressed by myself, thank you." He insisted at least on that much.

"You've broken your kneecap, Mr. Shackelford," Dr. Brown said solemnly after looking intently at the x-rays. "We're going to try to avoid surgery, but that means absolutely no pressure on that knee for a full six weeks."

"Uh-huh." *I am not going to just sit around and watch the grass grow. I have work to do—ball games to attend!*

"He can walk on crutches though, right?" Jo asked. Luke knew she was trying to reach some compromise.

Dr. Brown shook her head. "Not for a while. I'm going to put his leg in a soft cast, but I want him to stay off of it completely for a full week. Mr. Shackelford, you can get up to go to the bathroom, using the crutches, but that's it. Then we'll see how you're doing, and maybe you can use them to do some very minimal activity until it heals."

With a set in his jaw, Luke shot a glance at his wife. He had no intention of obeying those orders if they meant missing Brianna's game.

Jo took a long breath, and Luke saw in her face she knew just what he was thinking. As soon as the doctor left the room, she gave him a stern look of her own. "Oh no you're not, don't even think about it. You'll stay home and rest that leg if I have to tie you to your recliner."

The ride home was not a fun one. They spent the entire time arguing about what he was going to do or not do that evening.

"I'll have someone videotape it and bring it to you as soon as the last buzzer sounds," Jo offered. But Luke knew he had leverage here.

"Oh, this from the woman who just two weeks ago

dragged herself to a game in spite of a hundred-and-three-degree fever," Luke said with a smirk and a dose of good-natured sarcasm. "I'm not the only one around here who won't take no for an answer."

✳

Sitting in the living room, leg propped up on the ottoman, Luke took up the argument again. "Jo, this is not just about my being stubborn," he said for probably the fiftieth time that day. "You know how important it is to Brianna that we both be there." But he could see that Jo wasn't budging.

"You heard the doctor's orders. She said NO pressure on your leg. You'd never get into the gym without being jostled or putting weight on it somehow. And where would you sit if you got there? I can't carry you up the bleachers."

"They have handicapped seating you know—" That's it! Why hadn't he thought of that before? "I'll get a wheelchair!" Yes. He'd found a way. "Do we know anyone with an extra wheelchair?"

"Luke, the doctor said for you not to go *anywhere*, and no, we don't know anyone with an extra wheelchair."

"Will you please just bring me the phone book?"

A few minutes later, however, Luke was more discouraged than ever. "I've called all the medical supply rental stores in the phone book, and they're either closed for the day or don't have any more wheelchairs available."

Jo let out a sigh, but this time he detected more sympathy than exasperation. "Dear, Brianna will understand. You're injured. She'll know you'd be there if you could."

"I know, but I wanted her to understand that I'd never break a promise to her." It was six o'clock. The game started at seven, and Luke was feeling like a prisoner in his own home.

"Look, your favorite team is playing on TV," Jo said. Luke knew she was trying to help. But tonight that wasn't going to be enough.

"Jo, even the Oklahoma State Cowboys couldn't distract me this evening." He sighed, finally ready to admit to defeat, when he suddenly had another idea. "Jo! Quick, bring me the phone again."

Her eyes narrowed, and she gave him a wary look as she handed him the phone. "What are you trying now?"

"Just watch and see," he said with a grin.

"Josh, hey, it's Pap. What are you doing right now?"

"Jake and I are getting ready to go watch Brianna's game," his grandson answered. "Hey, sorry about your knee. Are you watching Oklahoma State play tonight?"

"Of course not," Luke retorted. "I'm going to Brianna's game."

"I thought you had doctor's orders to stay off that knee," Josh said.

"I do—that's where you and Jake come in. I need two strong young men to carry me into the game." Luke looked over to his wife. She just shook her head, threw her hands in the air, and walked away. He smiled, knowing she'd forgive him before the evening was over.

"We'll be there in no time," Josh said.

❋

Luke heard the chants of cheerleaders and the thumps of basketballs as he rode into the gymnasium on the arms of his two grandsons. He didn't care how old or feeble he looked, he was just glad to be there and to have kept his promise.

He settled gingerly into the chair they'd brought from home and managed to catch Brianna's eye as she warmed up. The look of surprise on her face was worth his every effort. She ran over and gave him a big hug.

Wouldn't Miss It

"What are you doing here?"

"I promised you I'd come—I wouldn't miss it for the world," he said with a smile.

Brianna shook her head and scolded, reminding him of Jo. But she was also transparent like her grandmother, and he could see that she was pleased. "I love you," she said, adding sternly, "but promise me you won't jump up and down when I score all the points." She flashed him a grin and jogged back onto the court. Just before she was out of range, she turned and called over her shoulder. "I knew you wouldn't miss it!"

Sharing Memories

chapter seven

Sharing Memories

Today is a day for
rejoicing! Think about
what's good, noble, and
right. Reflect on things
that are pure, lovely,
and admirable. Anything
excellent or praiseworthy
warrants memories.
Meditate on all I've done
for you, and consider all
My mighty deeds.

Remembering you,
Your God of Joy

—from Psalm 118:24; Philippians 4:8; Psalm 77:12

A one-year-old with her face covered in birthday cake. An elderly couple holding hands. A snuggly, fuzzy kitten. You can't help but smile at these things.

God gives us little gifts just like these every day to smile about—things that make us happy. Things that brighten our days. Good memories we can use to cheer ourselves and others. Look back at old photographs. You probably have some of these cheery memories stored away in a box. Maybe you're grinning just thinking about them. Where's that picture of your five-year-old when he discovered the puppy Santa put in his stocking, or the one of your oldest daughter painting her sister's toenails? How about the one of you and your husband running through a cascade of rice, eager to start your life together?

Sometimes our days can get lonely, or tiresome, or too hectic. But if we pay attention, we'll see that God is sprinkling little blessings in our lives. If you feel like you haven't experienced one of these recently, pull out those old photo albums and spend some time remembering.

Life is full of memories—some good, some not so good. Stay focused on the good ones and let the difficult times get a little faded. Then take some of that happiness and the empathy you learned along the way, and share them with others who might need some comfort or just some company. Before you know it, the day will be filled with smiles—yours and theirs.

God gave us memories
that we we might have
roses in December.

❋

J. M. Barrie

No one had ever knocked on Trudy's door before. It was the sweetest sound she'd heard in a long time.

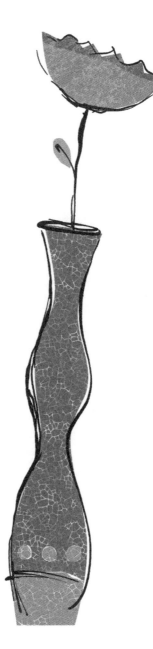

Company

The year was 1962, and Jim and Trudy had only been married four months when Jim proudly announced, "I got a job in North Carolina for the summer. We move in two weeks."

The nineteen-year-old newlyweds had been living in an apartment over Trudy's parents' garage while they were both in college, so they were excited about embarking on this great adventure. Trudy looked forward to having her own place and being the perfect housewife. She happily envisioned Jim coming home from a hard day at work to a clean apartment and a beautiful meal she had lovingly prepared.

Since they didn't own a car and couldn't afford a moving van, they decided to set out for their new home by train. They took only what they could fit in a couple of suitcases, but that didn't bother them. All they needed was each other.

A month after being in North Carolina, however, Trudy was lonely. Jim worked twelve-hour shifts at the plant, so she was alone much of the time. She lived for the weekends, when Jim was off and they would picnic and explore the countryside together. But the weekdays just seemed to creep by. She did laundry on Mondays, vacuuming and dusting on Tuesdays, and grocery shopping almost every day, trying to spread out her chores.

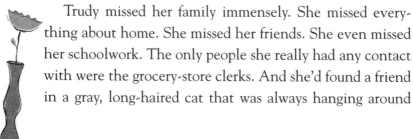

Trudy missed her family immensely. She missed everything about home. She missed her friends. She even missed her schoolwork. The only people she really had any contact with were the grocery-store clerks. And she'd found a friend in a gray, long-haired cat that was always hanging around the store. The cat had friendly blue eyes, and Trudy enjoyed when it would rub against her legs as she walked through the door. She always stooped to say hello and to stroke its silky fur.

Trudy walked the three-fourths of a mile to the grocery store even when she didn't need to buy much—or anything at all. She'd spend at least an hour combing the aisles, making small talk with anyone who would join in. "Those cantaloupes look nice and ripe, don't they?" she would ask. She received polite smiles and a few brief replies but never the conversation she longed for.

One day as she stood in the check-out lane, the middle-aged man Trudy guessed was the owner of the small market approached her.

"Excuse me, ma'am, I'm George. I've noticed that you come here often and always carry your bag home."

Trudy was thrilled just to have someone else initiate an exchange, and this man reminded her of her dad, who called all ladies "ma'am" no matter how old or young they were. "Yes sir, I live less than a mile from here. My husband and I don't have a car, so I make frequent small trips and get just what I can carry."

"I'd be glad to let you borrow a grocery cart if you need

it," he offered politely. "My wife could come by your place later and pick it up."

She was excited about the opportunity for some company. At last, maybe she could make a new friend. Trudy didn't really need enough groceries to fill a cart, but she wasn't about to pass up this gracious offer. She thanked him profusely and proceeded to stroll up and down the aisles, buying anything she thought she could use.

She felt a little odd pushing a grocery cart down the sidewalk, but she didn't care. It was a change of pace in her long, monotonous week. She wasn't sure what she would do tomorrow, since she now had enough groceries to last for a while, but she'd figure that out later.

Right now she had big plans to bake a cake, one of those delicious sour-cream pound cakes her mom had taught her to make. She wanted to be prepared for her first visitor.

Later Trudy started when she heard the rap of the doorknocker. No one had ever knocked on her door before, and she was sure it was the sweetest sound she'd heard in a long time. She quickly scanned the tiny apartment to make sure everything was in place, then ran to greet her guest.

"Hi, please come in," she said to the woman with the kindest face she'd ever seen. "I'm Trudy. I'm so glad you came."

Company

"My name is Betty, and it's my pleasure," the store owner's wife said with a smile. She placed the basket she was carrying gently on the floor beside the sofa and took a long, gratifying whiff of the aroma coming from the kitchen. "Something smells wonderful!"

Trudy beamed with pride. "It's my mother's special pound cake. Would you like some? I was hoping you'd sit down and have a piece with me."

Betty sat on the old couch that had come with the apartment as Trudy served her the cake and some tea. "This brings back fond memories of when George and I were first married," she said sweetly.

They chatted awhile, Trudy devouring stories of George and Betty's newlywed life and sharing

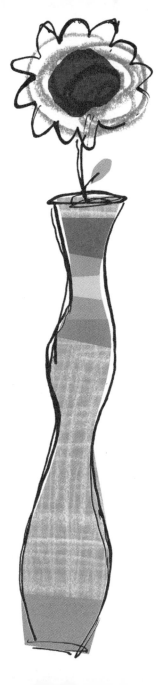

some of her own. Betty told about meals she had burned, once even setting off the smoke alarm, and about their first move away from home. "It was so hard to leave my family and friends to go where I didn't know anyone but my husband. He spent most of his time trying to earn a living for the two of us, and I felt terribly alone."

Before Trudy could catch herself, tears sprang to her eyes. Somehow it felt soothing to know someone else had felt as she did now.

"George told me he's seen you in the store almost every day. He asked me to pick up the cart and to bring you a little something. It's been more than a few years, but we do remember how it is to be newlyweds and far away from home."

Betty went on to tell Trudy that they had lived in a similar little apartment and that one day, to her surprise and delight, their landlord had broken one of her own rules and had given her a little gray kitten named Sweet Pea to keep her company. "That kitten had the most friendly blue eyes and was the best little friend to me."

Suddenly making the connection, Trudy gasped. "It can't be. The nice cat from the store?" Did cats live that long?

114

Company

"Oh, so you've met Dolly. No, she's Sweet Pea's great-great-granddaughter. Sweet Pea's family has grown right along with ours, and that kind landlord became a lifetime friend of the family too." As Betty talked, she picked up the basket and slowly pulled back a blanket to reveal a beautiful, tiny, fuzzy, gray kitten curled up and sound asleep.

"Dolly had kittens just six weeks ago. When George told me about you, we agreed right away that you were just the person we wanted to have one of her precious babies—to pass on this blessing of friendship. We wouldn't give her to just anyone."

"Oh! She's beautiful! I'd love to have her. I promise I'll take very good care of her," Trudy gushed, her voice filled with gratitude.

Betty chuckled as she got up to leave. "I know you will. It's always nice to have someone to talk to when you're far away from home. Even if that someone doesn't talk back." She smiled warmly.

"Thank you so much," Trudy said as she kissed her new furry companion on the back of her neck. "And please, Betty, come back again—and here, take a piece of pound cake for your husband. This was so kind of you both."

That night when Jim arrived home, Trudy was curled contentedly on the sofa with the little gray kitten purring happily on her lap. They named her Ally, and she became like a member of the family. George and Betty became like Jim and Trudy's parents away from home, inviting them over often for Sunday lunch during their few months there.

Several years had passed when Trudy walked up the stairs carrying a covered basket. She could hardly contain her smile as she knocked on the apartment door. The stairs weren't as easy to climb as they used to be, and the memories were almost overwhelming when she was greeted by a smiling young woman she'd met at church the previous Sunday.

Company

"Please, come in! It's so nice to have some company," she said. "I never realized how lonely it would be moving to a new town all alone."

Trudy entered and gently placed the basket on the floor, hoping the little gray kitten would sleep until she was ready to pull back the blanket.

Look for these other great Hugs™ books